This Is My Home, Lord
A Woman's Prayers

Books by same author
  CHRISTIAN MARRIAGE (Mowbray)
  GOING THE JESUS WAY (Scripture Union)
  WHY GET MARRIED? (Mowbray)

This Is My Home, Lord

A Woman's Prayers

by Helen Lee

Foreword by Brenda Blanch

Winston Press, Inc.
430 Oak Grove
Minneapolis, MN 55403

Copyright © 1982 by Helen Lee.

Originally published in Great Britain by A. R. Mowbray & Co. Ltd. This edition is published by Winston Press, Inc., by arrangement with A. R. Mowbray & Co. Ltd. All rights reserved. No part of this book may be reproduced in any form without written permission from the publisher.

Library of congress Catalog Card Number: 82-51245
ISBN: 0-86683-683-7 (previously ISBN: 0-264-66856-1)

Printed in the United States of America
5   4   3   2   1

Cover design: Tom Egerman
Cover photo: Nancy Bundt

Bible references marked GNB are taken from the *Good News Bible* — Old Testament: copyright © American Bible Society 1976; New Testament: copyright © American Bible Society 1966, 1971, 1976.
Bible references marked RSV are taken from the *Revised Standard Version* of the Bible, copyrighted 1946, 1952, © 1971, 1973. Used by permission.
Bible references marked AV are taken from the *King James Version* of the Bible.

Winston Press, Inc.
430 Oak Grove
Minneapolis, MN 55403

FOREWORD

For many of us the word Home conjures up visions of warmth and love, a place where you can relax and be yourself – in fact, a place where you can feel 'at home'. But all of us who have homes to run and families to care for know that someone has to act as pivot if the place is to remain a home, and being the pivot is not always a comfortable position. We become all too aware of other people's problems and of our own inadequacies, and can feel very alone.

In these prayers Helen Lee reveals some of the burdens and joys that have come her way as the creator of a home, and how she has coped with them. When I was a very new Christian I used to long to be able to live for a while with other Christians, so that I could discover how they lived. These prayers would have helped me. They will help you, too. You will discover that you are not alone in your turmoil, that someone else feels just as you do, and I hope that the prayers may help you to find new strength each day in Christ.

Brenda Blanch

DEDICATION

For Bill,
for our family,
and for all who have shared our home.

CONTENTS

Foreword page v

PART ONE: INSIDE MYSELF

    This is my home, Lord 8
    I've got to say Thankyou, Lord 10
    At a time of stress at home 12
    Keeping going 14
    Feeling sorry for myself 16
    Recovery 18
    Not for tomorrow, Lord 20
    Listening 22
    About having enough 24
    Growing older 26
    Gladness 28
    Trying and failing 30
    Unkindness 32
    Troubled by doubts 34
    A prayer for New Year's Eve 36

PART TWO: MY FAMILY

    A child starting school 40
    Lord I have been so angry 42
    A daughter growing up 44

For my husband 46
Tested by separation 48
A birthday 50
A child's disappointments 52
The questions children ask 54
Grandparents 56
Teen Years 58

PART THREE: HOME HAPPENINGS

Flowers in the house 62
Polishing 64
Suffering 66
A prayer at night 68
A hot bath 70
The telephone 72
A party 74
Sowing 76
Something lost 78
Empty house 80
For a sick animal 82
A new baby in the home 84
The shadow of your hand 86

PART FOUR: THE WORLD OUTSIDE MY DOOR

Going out to work 90
Friends 92
Crime in the streets 94
Holidays away 96
The homeless and hungry 98
Snow 100
Neighbours 102
A journey 104
When the news is bad 106

Broken families *108*
Shopping *110*
Schools and teachers *112*
The hesitation *114*
Moving house *116*

Index of Bible References

PART ONE

Inside Myself

This is my home, Lord

This is my home, Lord:
fill it with your peace.
Make it a haven for discouraged hearts,
make it a fortress against lovelessness
and greed and self-conceit.
May its simplicity
speak of the wealth of all that we possess
in having you to share our home with us.
Help us to recognise each other's thoughts
and fears and hopes and personalities.
Give me enough –
but just enough, my Lord –
to keep the daily needs supplied,
enough to eat, enough to clothe us with,
and strength enough to lift and clean and bake.
And give us laughter, kind and generous,
music,
the sounds of people having fun,
and open-hearted talk.
But let there be a quietness sometimes,
the space to read and pray and rest myself,
stillness – the music for a weary head.

This is my home, Lord:
use it as you will,
its strengths and privacy and all it holds.
Only be here with me each night and day,
here at our mealtimes,
with me while I work,
here at the day's beginning and its end,
here while we sleep.

Psalm 27.4–5

I have asked the Lord for one thing; one thing only do I want: to live in the Lord's house all my life, to marvel there at his goodness, and to ask for his guidance.
In times of trouble he will shelter me; he will keep me safe in his Temple and make me secure on a high rock. *(GNB)*

I've got to say Thankyou, Lord

I've got to say *Thankyou*, Lord.
I'm not much good at words
but deep inside myself
I want to praise and sing.
The smell of rain in the garden lifted my
 morning.
The postman brought me
friendship renewed and warming.
The children brought home gifts from school,
grubby trophies of concentration
proudly presented. Thankyou, Lord.
The baking turned out right
(won through anxiety and heat!)
and we've had laughter, family gales of it.

And all of us at home
are well in body and soul
(and mostly sleeping now – thankyou my
   Lord!)
For all these things and countless others
that stir my heart and lift my tired spirits
I want to sing.
But thankyou more than all
for being *you*, my never-failing one,
friend at the heart's core, friend at the day's end,
friend of the failure and the rebel,
friend of mine.

Psalm 34.1–3

I will always thank the Lord; I will never stop praising him. I will praise him for what he has done; may all who are oppressed listen and be glad! Proclaim with me the Lord's greatness; let us praise his name together! (GNB)

At a time of stress at home

Father just look at us!
As taut as bow-strings, eyeing each other.
We have let fly the bitter words,
this way and that way, all of us involved;
we have seen the turned shoulder and the hard
    young mouth,
have heard the door slam.
and now the hostile silence
full of unspoken things;
and all over nothing, Father,
trivial foolishness.
But each of us is hurt, how hurt you only know.
Where will it lead? Where will it end?
Must I apologise?
I didn't cause it, Lord, I only tried
to be a peace-maker and blundered in
and made it worse.

Yes, yes, I know, my Lord,
Someone must build the bridge.
And hurt and wretchedness and humble pie
Are all the cost of love.
Now that I'm still and hear you speak,
I hear you say
your love was crucified.

So help me Jesus,
give me words and actions now
to be the first
to build a bridge of love.

Psalm 46.10
Be still and know that I am God. (RSV)

Keeping going

I don't feel proud of anything, Lord.
I can hardly hold up my head.
But I must.
I've got to keep going for everyone's sake,
and my body will scarcely do the things
    I tell it to.
Lord this is a cry for help.

Don't let the devil have his way with me:
help me to do the necessary things,
give me the confidence to lift my eyes
beyond the impossible now.
And yes –
make me aware of Jesus' power in me
more than all else.

2 Corinthians 12.9

My grace is sufficient for you, for my power is made perfect in weakness. *(RSV)*

Feeling sorry for myself

Lord I must just sit down and talk to you.
There are stacks of greasy dishes by the sink,
and the vacuum cleaner's dead,
and I feel so tired, *tired*.
Tired of the endless chores, and
    balancing money
against demand.
Tired of demands,
tired of being taken for granted.
Were you ever taken for granted, Lord?
My God, of course you were!
Each day I breathe
I take you for granted.
Jesus was left to agonise alone
while the others slept –

Deal with my burden of resentfulness;
wipe clean self-pity;
set my mainspring right;
help me to see
that work is love in action,
your love, my hands.
So when the boredom and the tension lift
I shall have strength to toil.
And now for the greasy pots, Father —
Stay by me, will you? while I run the tap . . .

Luke 10.40–42

Martha was upset over all the work she had to do, so she came and said, 'Lord, don't you care that my sister has left me to do all the work by myself? Tell her to come and help me!'
The Lord answered her, 'Martha, Martha! You are worried and troubled over so many things, but just one thing is needed.' (GNB)

Recovery

God, you were speaking to a nation;
to a whole generation of people;
to the church across the world.
Even the weight of the whole weary world
is nothing to you.
But your words reach home to me,
comforter, healer of pain,
even to me.
The weakness I felt so little time ago
is lifted and gone.
I want to thank you, life within my life.
For all recovery
all wholeness and well-being,
all strength in weakness, all sustaining power
    come
only from you.
They are the breath of your vitality.

Now I can walk and work and sing and laugh
because you've lifted me
and made me whole . . .
And here before I take another step
I want to thank you, Lord.

Isaiah 40.29–31

He strengthens those who are weak and tired. Even those who are young grow weak; young men can fall exhausted. But those who trust in the Lord for help will find their strength renewed. They will rise on wings like eagles; they will run and not get weary; they will walk and not grow weak. *(GNB)*

Not for tomorrow, Lord

Not for tomorrow, Lord,
just for today,
strength to get through the nursing and the
 chores,
to climb the stairs and carry trays,
to smile and answer gently and support:
this I am asking for.
It's been a long night, Father, and I carry
the load alone.
Today's another day with no relief,
no walking in the garden, looking round the
 shops,
meeting a friend.
But you have promised to be with me Lord,
here where I am,
here where my back aches and self-pity wells.

You never leave me, never left me yet.
So bless my sick one, Father,
and bless me.
Give us both strength and cheerful fortitude
just for today.

2 Corinthians 12.9

My grace is sufficient for you, for my strength is made perfect in weakness. (RSV)

John 12.26

My servant will be with me where I am. (GNB)

1 Chronicles 4.23

They dwelt there with the king for his work.
(RSV)

Listening

Father I talk too much.
Clamour and plead and argue, even to you,
    my Lord.
Teach me to have a stillness in my soul,
time to be quiet, here in your quiet presence.
Waken my ear to listen, as you have
Isaiah's, Paul's, and many another one.
The world goes screaming round my head,
music, traffic, voices, machinery;
let me not add my clamour to the rest,
but deep within myself
let there be stillness Lord.
So may I have a ready ear to hear
all those who want to tell me something; friends
or family, or someone in the road.

Make me not only still enough to listen
but ready with that quiet sustaining word
that helps in weariness,
or lifts anxiety, perhaps distils
a drop of wisdom even.
Give me a listening ear.

Isaiah 50.4

The Lord has given me the tongue of those who are taught, that I may know how to sustain with a word him that is weary. Morning by morning he wakens, he wakens my ear to hear as those who are taught. (RSV)

About having enough

Thankyou my God for being enough for me:
thankyou that you never fail
to make me rich when I come back to you
with empty hands.
Sometimes I hanker for more that money would
   buy,
feel jealous of my neighbours and the things
they can afford. Forgive me Father
for I have enough.
Too many goods would weigh me down with
   care,
too much of sweetness sicken my taste,
too fast a pace of pleasure would leave me out of
   breath
for all I have to do,
and still not satisfied.

So help me to rejoice in all you give,
the rich variety of each day's joys,
the infinite flavour of simplicity,
the daily needs well met, the bonuses,
the money that I have – to spend and save and
 give.
I pray for wisdom in the spending,
love in the giving,
and for gratefulness.
And thankyou Father that you are enough.

1 Timothy 6.17

Command those who are rich in the things of this life not to be proud, but to place their hope, not in such an uncertain thing as riches, but in God, who generously gives us everything for our enjoyment. (GNB)

Growing older

Father I haven't come to terms
with growing old.
My heart, my thoughts, my loving and my
    dreams
are just the same as when I stood and looked,
with eyes newly mature, at the long vista of the
    coming years.
I haven't changed, and yet my body has.
Sometimes it aches with tiredness; and the
    clothes
I loved to wear don't suit me any more.
The mirror shows me lines around my face
that makeup will not hide.
Lord, help me not to fight with growing old,
resent it, hate myself.
Give me a brave and joyful spirit, go
along with me through every fresh new day
with your glad company.

Give me the strength for *all you'd have me do*,
sufficient just for that.
And may the lines upon my face
be lines of laughter and of deep concern
for others' sadnesses;
not lines of anger or self-pity, nor
of bleak anxiety. Make me a strength
within my family, among my friends,
a quiet source of your encouragement,
Because you care for me.

Isaiah 46.4

I am your God and will take care of you until you are old and your hair is grey. I made you and will care for you; I will give you help and rescue you.
(*GNB*)

Gladness

Father there were finches
outside my window just now.
Alight with happiness, bursting with song, the
 sunlight
gold on their wings.
Thankyou
that they made me stop my work a minute
and look up.

I can't grasp all the happiness and beauty
and rightness that are you, Lord, but I can see
finches and sunshine,
and recognize the beauty of your making.
Thankyou for gladness.

Psalm 118.24

This is the day which the Lord has made; let us rejoice and be glad in it. (RSV)

Genesis 1.25

God made them all, and he was pleased with what he saw. (GNB)

Trying and failing

Father I feel frustrated with myself.
Nothing I do turns out
the way I hoped it would:
the dress I make, the room I decorate,
the special cake I bake,
they all go wrong in varying degrees
however hard I try.
But worse than this,
I sometimes spoil relationships
by blundering or forgetfulness, or just
by over-haste and lack of thoughtfulness.
God when you make a thing
you make it perfect, and yet some of us,
your creatures,
make nothing but mistakes.

Help me to face the fact
that I'm a blunderer, yet one
that you still love.
Help me to think afresh
how Jesus came
just for the sake of those who fail like me,
fall short of even what they want to be
and make a mess of life.
Thankyou that Jesus came to make us whole.

Psalm 145.13–14

The Lord is faithful to his promises, and everything he does is good.
He helps those who are in trouble; he lifts those who have fallen. (GNB)

Unkindness

Dear God I've got to tell
someone. Forgive me that it's you.
I've been misjudged, misunderstood,
    deliberately
misquoted, had the truth twisted,
had the tongues of gossips wag.
I've had my trusted friends speak ill of me,
and enemies rejoice to pass it on.
I've swung from anger to depression,
and to bitter hurt.
But Lord,
what's the use?
I want to hit back, to vindicate myself,
prove myself right; and like a child
I want to shout, '*It isn't fair.*'

But you who know what lies in all of us,
know all the truth of it.
No need to spell it out, or justify
myself to you, my God.
It's you who are the judge, and all my faults
already you've forgiven and wiped clean.
Forgive me this too, Lord,
that I've resented to the point of hate,
and in my wounded pride
I have let anger turn to bitterness.

Now that I've told you Lord I can be still,
and find again the peace
my sore heart needs.

John 14.27

'Peace I leave with you; my peace I give to you; not as the world gives do I give to you. Let not your hearts be troubled, neither let them be afraid.' (RSV)

Troubled by doubts

Lord Jesus, I am standing in the fog.
Nothing seems certain to me now, not even
  yourself.
The faith I've shared with others, with which
  I've propped
my family and husband all these years, has
  turned to mist.
The shapes of all my certainties have lapsed
into remote and insubstantial shadows.
Now in the crisis of anxiety
when most I'm needing to believe,
doubt creeps and clings around me like a fog.
But thankyou Lord
that I don't need to force my doubting mind
to blot out every possibility
of anything that I believed not being so;
or trust against all probability
that prayer will have its answer, neat, exact,
as I have prayed it.

Thankyou Jesus
that all I need to trust is *you yourself*,
and I can stand
here in my fog of doubts
and wait to see you roll the mists away.
Lord I believe – so feebly, so much less
than I should do – but help my unbelief!

Mark 9.22–24

'If you can do anything, have pity on us and help us.' And Jesus said to him, 'If you can! All things are possible to him who believes.'
Immediately the father of the child cried out and said, 'I believe; help my unbelief!' (RSV)

A prayer for New Year's Eve

God, I'm oppressed by all I meant to do
in this past year, and failed,
the way I've wasted time.
Time chases me relentlessly and saps my
    strength –
another year has disappeared behind me.
Yet something has been gained:
you have made rich my home and the life here,
Lord; you have even sometimes
enabled us to be part of the richness of others.
My fears you have often turned into relief
when I caught up with them.
I know you a little better than I did,
your changeless, infinite patience and
    forgivingness.
There have been a few good milestones too,
small triumphs, and victories not so little
for those I love the best.
The New Year daunts me with the fears
of unknown possibilities,
yet comforts me because of fresh beginnings.

I'm so thankful God that time is nothing to you,
the end or the beginning, that you will never
grow old or tired, never get perplexed,
that nothing is too big or unexpected for you
to have grasped and overcome already.
Thank you that you have always been our
    home,
safe beyond measure or telling,
and so will always be.

Psalm 90.1–4

O Lord, you have always been our home. Before you created the hills or brought the world into being, you were eternally God, and will be God for ever.

You tell man to return to what he was; you change him back to dust.

A thousand years to you are like one day; they are like yesterday, already gone, like a short hour in the night. (GNB)

PART TWO

My Family

A child starting school

Lord, he's been so eager for this day,
and now it's come; and with new shoes, new
 cap, new pencil-case,
he has gone in alone.
So many people bigger than he,
so much bewildering rush.
Lord I can picture him, trying to be brave
and wishing it was time for home and tea.
Be with him, Father, keep him strong,
cheerfully facing life, trying his best.
Not just today, but all the future days
when he must go out beyond the known and
 safe,
and tackle problems with his own resource
and face the consequences on his own,
be with him Lord, and keep him in your hands.

Help me as well to let him be himself. I know
that from this day he'll never quite be mine.
He's taken today
the first step on the road that leads from home,
and I must stay and watch.
Deliver me from that possessiveness
that wants to smother and protect and keep.
Help me to let him go.

Psalm 127.3–4

Children are a gift from the Lord; they are a real
blessing. Sons . . . are like arrows. (*GNB*)

Lord I have been so angry

Lord I have been so angry with my son.
Angry to hitting rage that frightens me.
And he is young,
with big rebellious eyes,
wary of me, yet standing his ground,
defying me.

Three things I need Lord, need them quickly:
Forgive me for this rage;
it leaves me ashamed, exhausted;
heal me Father.
Help my young ruffian to collect himself,
to yield to wisdom (not to me, to me)
and give way (as he must) with dignity.

Then build the bridge between us as it was.
Help us to see each other with a fresh respect
and to be friends;
for hurts unhealed will fester and go deep.
Only you Lord can cleanse and heal and build,
Lord only you.

Mark 4.39

Jesus stood up and commanded the wind 'Be quiet!' and he said to the waves 'Be still!' The wind died down, and there was a great calm.

(GNB)

A daughter growing up

Dear God this child of yesterday
is growing up. This tomboy in her jeans and
 stripey shirt
is fast becoming woman.
Lovely she is to look at, tall, with boyish grace,
and full of mischief, moods, flashes of
 tenderness,
fits of laughter, fits of sulky silence.
It isn't easy, God, this growing up,
becoming woman.
There are so many magnets tugging at her heart,
and rocks and whirlpools and uncharted seas
lie all ahead of her.
And we who love her to distraction, cannot
 make
decisions for her. She must be herself,
and through mistakes and hurts and tears
come to maturity.
Please have her, Lord,
in your strong hands. Settle her young
 rebellious heart
towards the goal of You,
your love, your loveliness, to serve you with her
 life.

Please hold us too
within the quiet of your understanding peace,
and give us all the wisdom that we need
to be what she most needs,
this woman-child of ours.

John 17.3

Eternal life means knowing you, the only true God, and knowing Jesus Christ, who you sent.

John 17.15

'I do not ask you to take them out of the world, but I do ask you to keep them safe from the Evil One.' (GNB)

For my husband

He works so hard Lord, puts his heart and soul
into his job to get it right, gives us the best
he can provide.
Sometimes forgets to give us of himself.
Sometimes his homecoming
is when the sun comes out,
bonanza of delight. And other times
shadows of disappointment and anxiety
creep in before him and the house is grey.
But at the times when things are really bad,
when we are waiting for an ambulance,
or faced with mountain debts,
hit by a cancelled holiday,
crushed by a family death,
his strong arm round me keeps the flood tides
    back,
stops me from drowning in the sea of it.
Thankyou my Father for a man like this.
Thankyou for all the work we've shared,
    eventually
have seen completed,
all the splitting laughter that we've had,
and moments when we've stood together, moved
too deeply for a spoken syllable.
Worthy the company of kings, he is,
fit to stand shoulder-high with any man.

Lord bless him in his work and in his home,
protects his travelling and guard his tongue,
and keep his health, backbone of all our life.
Bless him, I pray, in grey anxiety
and in profound heart-places which I glimpse
only a little.
Bless him in all that he finds difficult,
and in the endless toil that each day brings,
and bless him in his special hours of happiness.

And make me fit
to be his right hand and his company,
to love him all ways and unstintingly,
to help when help is needed, and to know
when to be silent; make me fit, my Lord,
to be his wife.

Proverbs 22.29

Show me a man who does a good job, and I will show you a man who is better than most and worthy of the company of kings. (GNB)

Tested by separation

God, it is something I can never feel used to,
having my man long weeks away from home,
living with half my heart dragged out of me,
anxious for news,
lonely for company.
No-one to share things with at the day's end,
no-one to take the children off my hands while I
get supper, write a letter, run to shops.
No-one to tell me he's enjoyed a meal,
or hear me out
when I have something niggling in my head;
and bed-time's lonely and the morning empty
    still.
Yes, yes I know
I'm only one of many thousand wives
who have to live a half-divided life,
often bereft; even together-times
tensed by the sense of parting just ahead.
I know, I know,
he's got a useful, satisfying job; that being away
is part of it; I know he loves me, longs to share
    with me
the life he leads, misses me too.

But something in me stands rebellious:
it wasn't his job I married, but himself.
I want him here,
beside me in our home.
But thankyou Lord that you've been lonely too,
and know the bitterness
of separation from the ones you love
who've gone away from home.
And if it is the measure and the cost of love
to grieve the way I do,
then never let me just get used to it.

Hebrews 2.18

For because (Jesus) himself has suffered and been tempted, he is able to help those who are tempted. (RSV)

A birthday

Lord bless this birthday, may it mark a mile
walked in a pilgrimage of grace.
Crown with success
a year of patient effort and resolve
in classroom, games field, office, spare-time
　　labour,
workshop or university.
Thankyou for lessons learned and buoyant
　　hopes,
for energy and enterprise and fun.
May this fresh year
stretch and develop all the latent powers
that wait for stimulus and opportunity.

Protect, in these twelve months, from atrophy,
self-satisfaction, selfishness and greed.
Set sights upon the goal of serving you
each birthday, Lord, however many come;
and give your peace and favour
day by day,
however long or short the pilgrimage.

Numbers 6.24–26

May the Lord bless you and take care of you.
May the Lord be kind and gracious to you.
May the Lord look on you with favour and give
you peace. (*GNB*)

A child's disappointments

Oh God I wish I could have borne the blow
    myself,
and not have seen this childish face
with sad, hurt eyes,
uncomprehending grief.
What can I do when life seems quite unfair,
to make it juster?
How can stinging tears be comforted?
No compensation lies within my power
for this one thing she'd set her heart upon.
Dear God, I wish the loss were mine, not hers!

I could have braced myself to face it squarely
since I have had more years' experience
to prove that time will bring alternatives,
hope to redress the balance of despair.
But at this moment, Father,
as I share her pain,
help us to trust you; make the light shine;
make even disappointment turn to gain.
Give us a rainbow Lord.

Psalm 34.18

The Lord is near to those who are discouraged; he saves those who have lost all hope.   (GNB)

The questions children ask

'What did God stand on when he made the
 earth?'
my five-year-old with wondering eyes
asks as I'm piecing out material,
patterns and pins.
'I don't believe in miracles, do you?' –
Fifteen-year-old endorsed by Mr. Jones
at school.
Questions that need an answer,
test my faith,
and in my ignorance, drive me to doubt
and subterfuge.
Lord give me patience never to dismiss
the question of a seeking, childish mind;
give me the wisdom to know what to say,
and when I don't, the sense to ask of you.
Source of all wisdom, show me where to look
for the right answers to our questioning.

May the undergirding of my trust in you
be a firm foothold for my children's feet.
Questions we ask,
problems we have,
doubts still will shoulder us,
but this we know,
you hold the answers, see the inscrutable,
make plain to us
all that we need to know.

James 1.5–6

If any of you lacks wisdom, he should pray to God, who will give it to him; because God gives generously and graciously to all. But when you pray you must believe and not doubt at all. Whoever doubts is like a wave in the sea that is driven and blown about by the wind.   (*GNB*)

Grandparents

God bless all loving grandparents!
Bless them for stretching out their love to
 encompass
another generation, and for being
patient and gentle with fresh sympathy
all over again.
Bless them when they make a second home
to reinforce a child's security;
and when they resolutely close their lips
on criticism of parental management.
And bless them Lord for simply being there
when crises threaten, for their sharing of the
 blows.

But bless them also when they weary, when
    demands
are overtaxing and when patience fails;
help us to understand
and make allowances for lost resilience.
Help us to take their love with gratitude.
God make a rich experience of
    grandparenthood,
let them be fruitful in the fruits of love.

Psalm 92.12–15

The righteous flourish like the palm tree, and grow like a cedar in Lebanon. They are planted in the house of the Lord, they flourish in the courts of our God.

They still bring forth fruit in old age, they are ever full of sap and green, to show that the Lord is upright. (RSV)

Teen Years

Lord Jesus,
fire and temper these young, eager souls;
grip their imagination, be their delight and
 dream;
in reckless mischief be a rein to them,
in generous-hearted service be a spur.
You who have been a boy, a youth, a man,
know all the impulses to good, to idleness,
to secrecy, the longing to revolt against
 authority,
the need for love,
the growing into independent self-hood.
In your hands
I put these boys and girls.
Keep them from harm, and through the risks
 they take
make them mature; temptations they must face,
but keep them strong.
Let there be honesty
between themselves and older folk,
that each may hear the other with respect.

Teach us, Lord Jesus, through their eagerness,
all-giving, dauntless, free
from self-protective second thoughts.
Teach us their openness and readiness to share.
And save us, Jesus, from destroying these
by our mistrust, our adult doubts and cares,
world-weary selfishness, cold lack of faith.
Send them as fire-filled messengers for you:
whatever you command them, let them speak.

Jeremiah I.6–7

Then I said, 'Ah, Lord God! Behold I do not know how to speak, for I am only a youth.'
But the Lord said to me, 'Do not say, "I am only a youth"; for to all to whom I send you you shall go, and whatever I command you you shall speak.' (RSV)

PART THREE

Home Happenings

Flowers in the house

Father I want to thank you,
just thank you with my heart.
The February rain is running down the glass,
there's washing, scrubbing, painting to be done,
and the stove to be cleaned –
but I have flowers in the room,
a pool of sunlight,
drop of the love of God.
The gift of them has set the day alight,
the coolness as I fixed them into shape
and made a picture of them,
the faint garden scent.

So I must stand a minute and forget
the rain, the grime, the business of the day;
and love you for the beauty of my flowers,
and thank you, Lord.

Song of Solomon 2.10–12

My beloved speaks and says to me: 'Arise, my love, my fair one, and come away; for the winter is past, the rain is over and gone. The flowers appear on the earth, the time of singing has come.' (RSV)

Polishing

Thankyou, Father, for a cheerful heart.
I've polished the chairs, the table and the floor,
polished the dusty window panes and made
a clear-way for the sun.
And though I'm hot and tired it was good.
Good to have work to do and strength to do it,
good to see light – your light – reflected
from all my worn and precious furniture.

More welcome still
it is, to sit with coffee cup
and see the sunshine touch the polished grains
and in their depth to catch the warm
smile of old friends.
For all my home I thank you, Lord,
and for a cheerful heart.

Proverbs 17.22

A cheerful heart is a good medicine, but a downcast spirit dries up the bones. (RSV)

Suffering

Lord, may my hands be your hands
as I lay them now
on this your suffering child.
Wholeness is part of you, comes from your
    loving will:
give wholeness now I pray, for body, soul and
    mind,
and make all three
contented with each other and with you.
Make whole the hidden places of the mind
and memories jagged aches, with your
    forgiveness;
lift the dull load of fear,
fear of tomorrow's pain, of dread disease, of
    surgery, of death;
give deep renewing sleep;
put your fresh life in sinew, nerve and cell;
wrap in the healing comfort of your love,
and give your wholeness, Lord.

Healer of suffering bodies, troubled minds
and broken hearts, I pray
for all who cannot lift a praying gaze to you,
for all bereaved, numbed, shocked and stricken
    souls,
and all whose minds
are troubled by their own imaginings,
clouded from joy, disordered, ill at ease.
Lord in your graciousness be near to bless
your dear and suffering ones.

Luke 5.12–13

'Sir, if you want to, you can make me clean!' Jesus stretched out his hand and touched him. 'I do want to,' he answered. 'Be clean!' At once the disease left the man. (GNB)

A prayer at night

How like you Lord to give the gift of sleep!
Warm bath of comfort at the tired day's end,
a break of sweet forgetting
before tomorrow,
renewal of our drained and empty store
of needed energy.
And if I can't sleep, Father,
still I can lie in peace, glad of the safety,
glad that you care
for all the trivial fears that fill my mind.

Lord for all those who have nowhere to lie,
no rest of heart in this security,
who long with desperate intensity
for morning light,
I ask your mercy.
And among the crowds I daily meet,
make me a sharer of the peace you give,
Provider of Sleep.

Psalm 4.8

I will both lay me down in peace, and sleep: for thou, Lord, only makest me dwell in safety.

(*AV*)

A hot bath

Lord Jesus you know what it is,
the comfort of water.
Gritty and sore and sandal-worn your feet were
    often,
and then to paddle in the sea's warm edge,
or have them washed and towelled in
    someone's home
at journey's end –
the comfort of it!
Thankyou for this bath.

The privacy and peace, the warmth and ease
just for a few short minutes;
long enough
to cleanse the dirt, relax the tension, lift the
    spirit.
Thankyou more than all
for giving within my inmost, wrought-up self
cleansing and peace and infinite release,
Jesus my Lord.

John 13.3–5

Jesus knew that the Father had given him complete power; he knew that he had come from God and was going to God. So he rose from the table, took off his outer garment, and tied a towel round his waist. Then he poured some water into a basin and began to wash the disciples' feet and dry them with the towel round his waist.

(GNB)

The telephone

Lord there are times when helps
turn into hindrances!
This telephone which gives me vital links
with friends and family, in crises summons aid
of every kind,
today has robbed me of all quietness.
Each task I've started had to be laid down;
time, budgeted exactly, slipped away
in agonising lengths of pointless talk;
the clanging bell
jars on my nerves
with yet another threatened burglary
of time and mental strength.
I'm at the mercy of unlimited demands,
here, where I've shut the door to get work done.

Lord will you turn frustration into
generosity?
Now, for me, please?
Give me a tiny flicker of the grace
you had with thronging multitudes, who
    wouldn't let you go.
Help me to know that people matter,

and their small concerns – not insignificant to
    them –
need someone's care. And why not mine my
    Lord?
Dear Jesus, you were vulnerable
to all of us. Help me accept
some little piece of vulnerability.

Mark 6.31–34

There were so many people coming and going
that Jesus and his disciples didn't even have time
to eat. So he said to them, 'Let us go off by
ourselves to some place where we will be alone
and you can rest for a while.' So they started out
in a boat by themselves for a lonely place. Many
people, however, saw them leave . . .
When Jesus got out of the boat, he saw this large
crowd, and his heart was filled with pity for
them, because they were like sheep without a
shepherd. So he began to teach . . .   (GNB)

A party

Jesus who loved a family gathering,
and jokes and laughter,
whose friendship was a bubbling spring
of sympathy and kindliness and fun,
flowing to all alike,
pauper and prostitute and wealthy Pharisee,
come share the party that we'll have tonight.
May there be happiness
with no faint undercurrent of unspoken spite;
and may this home
have all the welcome of your presence here;
save us from false politeness;
may heart-warm friendliness be in our words
and looks and actions, as we bid our guests
    come in.
And when they go,
may they feel inwardly at peace, content.

Please may there be
enough of food and drink,
neither too ostentatious nor too plain,
enough to tell our friends and neighbours that
we hold them dear, and love their company.
So when it's over, and we clear the room,
wash up the glasses, gather up the crumbs,
may we rejoice that you too were our guest,
and still we have
your glowing company.

John 2.1–2

There was a wedding in the town of Cana in Galilee. Jesus' mother was there, and Jesus and his disciples had also been invited to the wedding ... (GNB)

Matthew 22.2

'The kingdom of heaven is like this. Once there was a king who prepared a wedding feast for his son ...' (GNB)

Sowing

Wet earth warmed by a film
of March sunshine,
and a pinch of seeds in the palm of my hand –
each one a minor miracle!
Parsley and peas and carrots, beans and
    cabbages,
wrapped in the tiny package of a seed.
Thankyou for each of them, in prospect now,
food for my family and friends and me.
Lord you have told us 'Ask for daily bread,'
and this I do, and trust, and plant my seeds.

God bless the soil
and bless
the warming sun, and stir to life
the hidden growth in every wizened husk;
and as we eat, then may we not forget
to thank the one who made seeds grow
to meet our daily needs.

Psalm 65.10–11

You soften the soil with showers and cause the young plants to grow. What a rich harvest your goodness provides! (GNB)

Something lost

Lord I have lost something,
and just because it's lost
I want it more than anything. I've searched,
    researched,
turned out the impossible places and the
    obvious,
wasted precious hours without reward.
God, calm the frantic whirling of my mind
and make me still enough to recollect
the day it last was underneath my hand,
and where to look afresh.
Or still enough to see
that it is not so indispensable
as now I think; that I can do without.
Father you know both where it is,
my missing treasure, my necessity,
and what it feels like to have treasures lost.

But your lost treasures are not trifling things
    like mine,
but people, infinitely precious folk.
All your yearning love
is in your search for them.
Forgive your child
for growing frantic over missing toys.

Luke 15.8–9

Suppose a woman who has ten silver coins loses one of them – what does she do? She lights a lamp, sweeps her house, and looks carefully everywhere until she finds it. When she finds it, she calls her friends and neighbours together, and says to them, 'I am so happy I found the coin I lost. Let us celebrate!' (GNB)

Empty house

O God my house is quiet now the children are
 gone,
Lonely. Empty. Hollow as a shell.
I go round tidying tidy rooms,
listening for homeward footsteps, feeling
that no-one needs my giving any more.
Yes, I have cried
over my empty house and empty heart.
Thankyou for knowing, Lord, and not
 despising.
Thankyou for being
here in the very place that seems so cold.
Thankyou for the healthy independence
that takes my children out to live their lives.

Thankyou for having them, as you have me,
safe in your keeping.
Help me to place
my love, my home, my skill and strength to
    serve,
afresh at your disposal.

John 14.18

'I will not leave you desolate; I will come to you.'
(RSV)

John 14.23

Jesus answered him, 'If a man loves me, he will keep my word, and my Father will love him, and we will come to him and make our home with him.' (RSV)

For a sick animal

I don't have to wonder if you care
about animals, dear God.
Jesus said so.
Marvellously you made them, and you love
 each one
with total understanding.
And my animals Lord,
you love them partly because they are part of
 me.
Please have my sick one in your careful hands
now as I pray.
I don't know how to help, or ease the pain.

Give the vet skill and kindness in his task.
I bring my load of sharp anxiety
to you, creator of all living things,
leave it with you.

Matthew 10.29

'For only a penny you can buy two sparrows, yet not one sparrow falls to the ground without your Father's consent.' (GNB)

A new baby in the home

Father what deep, mysterious,
magic discovery
is fatherhood and motherhood.
You've shared with us a breath of your own joy
in making life. Gorgeous this baby is,
gift of your love, miraculous as all your gifts.

Thankyou for life and personality,
the skills and strengths, courage, imagination,
achievements, fun,
that lie in the crook of my arm.
His downy head, dark eyes and curling fingers
take my breath away.

Whatever time holds for him, Father,
pain or delight,
you know the end from the beginning;
his needs are already your care.
Let your service, Lord, be his fulfilment,
your company the joy of his journey,
yourself the goal and the arrival,
as the beginning.

1 Samuel 3.26–28

'Do you remember me? I am the woman you saw standing here, praying to the Lord. I asked him for this child, and he gave me what I asked for. So I am dedicating him to the Lord. As long as he lives, he will belong to the Lord.' (GNB)

The shadow of your hand

Lord, what is this stillness called death?
Every day people die, their names in the papers,
their spaces filled by others,
and I accept it. Part of life, inevitable end.
But now, today, I'm face to face with death
in one I know and love,
someone who yesterday
was thinking living thoughts, was real and here.
And now this stillness, like an empty house,
its owner gone. No words, no thoughts.
God, I feel lonely,
baffled and frightened at what I don't
    understand.
Part of my childhood, part of *me* is dead,
the wind blowing over the grass has blown
over me too.

Lord in the blankness and the emptiness
thankyou for this:
that your love holds us fast through life and in
 the stillness
that we call death, and in the life that lies
ahead of death.
Thankyou that your hands
hold both of us equally.
Thankyou for knowing all and understanding
 all,
and being the Father who lifts his tired children
at the day's end and carries them home.
Thankyou that death is nothing
but the shadow of your hand.

Psalm 103.15–17

As for man, his days are like grass; he flourishes
like a flower of the field; for the wind passes over
it, and it is gone, and its place knows it no more.
But the steadfast love of the Lord is from everlasting to everlasting upon those who fear him, and
his righteousness to children's children.   (RSV)

PART FOUR

The World Outside My Door

Going out to work

Father I've joined the thronging crowds
of women who live two lives in one,
pressed by necessity to work and earn.
Give me the strength
to bear both burdens peacefully and well.
I love my home, dear Lord, my heart is here;
yet give me pride to do a useful job,
and put my other skills and gifts to work
to serve my fellow people.
So may I give my best to both my lives.

Let not my home be poorer for my being
not always there. God bless all those
who share the care of house and home with me,
the meals, the children and the home-making,
and thankyou for them.
Bless my family:
help us to grow the closer for the separate ways
   we take
when Monday morning summons us to work.

Isaiah 26.3

Thou dost keep him in perfect peace, whose mind is stayed on thee, because he trusts in thee.
(RSV)

Friends

Thankyou, Father, for my friends,
for all their kindess (undeserved, incredible)
the way they come to help me when the
    pressures mount –
forgetting their own;
the way their sympathy
softens the bitterness of things gone wrong.
Lord they have cooked us meals, minded the
    children,
got on their knees, mended and cleaned and
    nursed,
and when there was nothing they could do,
they gave their company with silent love
which spoke to me of you,
Friend beyond all.

With all my heart I want
to be a friend, good and reliable
and quick to notice need,
to all of those I meet who want
my friendship, Lord,
and yours.

Proverbs 27.10

Your friend, and your father's friend, do not forsake; and do not go to your brother's house in the day of calamity. Better is a neighbour who is near than a brother who is far away. (RSV)

Matthew 11.19

Behold . . . a friend of tax-collectors and sinners. (RSV)

Crime in the streets

God there seems no safety any more;
we dare not trust the stranger at the door,
even in daylight violence is rife,
and our familiar walks, the shops, the carpark
    and the bus shelter
are settings for dishonesty,
and filthy words daubed up to assail the mind,
and vandalism, hall-mark of the lost.
So I am crying to you Lord,
defend the old and frail along our road,
protect the children from perverted minds,
and shield *their* minds, O God, from all the
    insidious slime.

When we go out at night, as go we must,
may we be confident within your care,
knowing that nothing touches us
unless by your consent.
O guard our children when they walk alone,
Protector of the helpless and the small;
and guard our door from evil,
mighty God.

Psalm 12.7–8

Do thou, O Lord, protect us, guard us ever from this generation. On every side the wicked prowl, as vileness is exalted among the sons of men.

(RSV)

Holidays away

A holiday Lord! a break from dull routine,
time to do nothing, time to climb and swim
and eat unhurried meals
by falling water underneath the sky,
time for the family, and time to talk.

The last week when the excitement boiled
I felt too harassed to want to go at all,
coping with packing, hassle,
thinking ahead.
But Jesus it was you
who told your friends to come away and rest,
knowing their serving, dogged working on,
hid their exhaustion.
So may I stop and gratefully accept
this gift of holiday.

Help us to take with wisdom all your gifts –
the recreation of our minds and souls,
the strength to work another working year,
family wholeness,
happiness,
Sunday refreshment from a different church,
and longer nights of deep renewing sleep.
Your gifts are always recreating, Lord.
Rest is the essence of your company;
rest is your gift.

Psalm 23.1–3

The Lord is my Shepherd; I have everything I need. He lets me rest in fields of green grass and leads me to quiet pools of fresh water. He gives me new strength. (GNB)

The homeless and hungry

No shelter from the rain,
or thieving hands; nowhere to keep
····possessions,
none to keep;
no supper and no bed, empty to lie
on cardboard or on rags; no self-respect;
no cleanness; no importance in society,
no matter to anyone until they die.
Dear God the earth holds thousands of your
····children thus,
unwanted, homeless, drifters on the tide;
and yet to you their worth is infinite,
and every separate life is your concern,
their misery
hangs on your heart; you long to gather them
and heal their brokenness.
Deliver us from hard complacency.
We have so much, my family and I –
save us from taking luxury as our right,

dismissing as an inconvenience
the crying needs of all your homeless ones.
Though all that we could do's
a trifling pittance in the face of poverty,
may chill indifference
not turn us back from doing what we can,
or rob our eyes and hearts of charity.
Have mercy on your world where greed and
    selfishness and poverty
go side by side.
Send help for homelessness.

Genesis 21.14–17

She left and wandered about in the wilderness of Beersheba. When the water was all gone, she left the child under a bush and sat down about a hundred metres away. She said to herself, 'I can't bear to see my child die.' While she was sitting there she began to cry. God heard the boy crying and from heaven the angel of God spoke to Hagar, 'What are you troubled about, Hagar? Don't be afraid. God has heard the boy crying.' (GNB)

Snow

How great you are, my Father, how immense
your sweeping majesty of silent snow!
The hills are wrapped in it. The towns are
    roofed with it.
You have blotted out the familiar garden,
    changed the shapes of trees and pavements
    and the neighbours' homes.
And still snow comes down ceaselessly
upon your noisy world, and hushes it.
And I have battled to weariness with
    shovelling,
battled with shopping and sodden shoes.
I have driven with fear and tension,
feared too for loved ones out upon the roads.
Thankyou for reminding me Father
of my own smallness, and helplessness
to govern my direction or keep safe my family.
Thankyou for hushing my noisy busyness. I
    cannot go,
I must be still.
Thankyou for your hands around
this beautiful and frightening world.

Have in your safe keeping Lord
all those who travel, those who struggle and are cold,
those who feel lost and travel on alone,
for Jesus's sake.

Job 38.22–30

'Have you entered the storehouses of the snow, or have you seen the storehouses of the hail, which I have reserved for the time of trouble, for the day of battle and war?
What is the way to the place where the light is distributed, or where the east wind is scattered upon the earth?
Who has cleft a channel for the torrents of rain, and a way for the thunderbolt, to bring rain on a land where no man is, on the desert in which there is no man;
to satisfy the waste and desolate land, and to make the ground put forth grass?
Has the rain a father, or who has begotten the drops of dew? From whose womb did the ice come forth, and who has given birth to the hoarfrost of heaven? The waters become hard like stone, and the face of the deep is frozen.' (RSV)

Neighbours

Father it's good to have
people around.
People who drop in, stay awhile, borrow and
 lend,
bring us their news, watch for the children,
 mind the house for us,
grow to be
a firm extention of our family.
Good to be needed by them in return;
and sometimes to supply their very want –
the grocery, the garden tool, the skill –
makes us feel rich to overflowing.
As our lives rub with theirs continually,
may each of us discover you afresh
in one another's generous company.
Help us to speak
with happy freedom of our trust in you,
and share the deepest joys and hopes we know,
since friends deserve the best we have to share;
but Lord may all we do
speak louder in your praise than what we say.
They see us in unguarded times, they know
our quick reaction to the unexpected blow,
 what lies behind the gracious smile.

They know.
So make them tolerant Father when we fail,
when we are noisy or discourteous,
take them for granted or forget our thanks.
And bless our neighbours for their being here
just when we need them, for reliability
and kindness and good sense. Without their
    love
how would we live? Make us good neighbours,
    Lord.

Galatians 6.2

Help to carry one another's burdens, and in this way you will obey the law of Christ. (GNB)

Romans 12.8

Whoever shares with others should do it generously ... whoever shows kindness to others should do it cheerfully. (GNB)

A journey

I need your help Lord: I've got to drive
an unfamiliar road, and find my way;
and traffic will be fast and heavy,
noisy, relentless.
Please keep us safe, my passengers and me;
help me to concentrate,
help me to show
gracious politeness to the impolite,
and more than that – kindness and courtesy
to those who wait
to join the stream, as I must sometimes wait.

Give me good judgement and good timing,
 please,
since other lives than mine depend on it,
and I can make mistakes. Yes Lord, I need
your strong protection in my journeying.

From Psalm 121

The protector of Israel never dozes or sleeps.
The Lord will guard you; he is by your side to protect you.
The Lord will protect you from all danger; he will keep you safe.
He will protect you as you come and go now and for ever. (GNB)

When the news is bad

Dear God the news is terrible today. It sickens
 me
to watch and hear it.
So much of it – the suffering and ugliness and
 pain –
come from our human greed and lovelessness,
our sordid minds.
Mine as well, Lord.
Even the family news
makes me sometimes anxious and ashamed.
Turn my eyes again to Jesus,
Jesus my Lord.
The vileness he met with, never made him vile,
although he took it, paid for it, bowed under it.
One day the news will have no sting in it:
when he takes charge, the news will be of *him*.

And even now
he reshapes human lives from human debris,
mess, and despair, and fragments of our wars:
I pray that you will grip my mind with that.
In my small world
make me a bringer of good news of him,
even if only with a look or smile, or reassuring
    word.
On this grey day
help me to lift another's heart,
to you my Lord.

2 Kings 7.9

We have good news and we shouldn't keep it to ourselves. (GNB)

Broken families

Mender and healer of broken things
since the beginning of recorded time,
I'm crying to you now
for all with broken hearts and broken homes,
and shattered dreams and bitter, angry
    thoughts.
Lord where the pressures dragged them down
or selfishness outweighed the love they had,
health failed,
or human blundering
brought to an end their hope of happiness,
give healing even there.
For children, lost, bewildered and betrayed,
their whole security bound in their parents's
    unity,
and lost –
God keep them in your love.

When I have seen a treasure fall,
splinter to fragments,
turn to waste,
Lord I have wept. The loss of one glass bowl
for me a small bereavement.
How much more to you
must be the broken treasure of a home,
a family, the centre of your love,
a gem that you had set your heart upon.

Psalm 31.9–10

Be merciful to me, Lord, for I am in trouble; my eyes are tired from so much crying; I am completely worn out. I am exhausted by sorrow ...
(GNB)

Psalm 16.5–6

You, Lord, are all I have, and you give me all I need; my future is in your hands. How wonderful are your gifts to me; how good they are! (GNB)

Shopping

Lord guard my eyes this morning when I go
out to the shops.
So *much* is lying there, spread on the shelves
before my face. Things I didn't need
before I saw them! Clothes that will catch my
    eye, and luxuries
we well could do without.
Please be the keeper of my purse today.
In your hand it will hold enough for us,
for all our needs, and bonuses besides.
Let me not squander what you give us Lord,
but spend it carefully with gratitude.

And in your keeping have my patience too;
may I be friendly with the shopkeepers,
and see the other women in the queue
as people with cares
people with ticking clocks and aching feet,
people like me.

When I have done,
and carried home my purse and purchases,
whether or not I bought the thing I sought,
make me content.

Matthew 6.20–21

Lay up for yourselves treasures in heaven, where neither moth nor rust consumes and where thieves do not break in and steal. For where your treasure is, there will your heart be also. (RSV)

Schools and teachers

O give them understanding hearts,
the teachers of our children;
give them authority with gentleness
and make them just;
help them not only to instruct
in English and Arithmetic and Art,
but to teach right-thinking and a love of all
    that's best
in the wide world; help them inspire
our children's curiosity to ask and learn and
    grow.
We give them lives to mould:
no diamond merchant handles richer gems,
no forester rears mightier giant trees,
no architect designs cathedral towers
more beautiful and splendid.

Lord bless and share with those who teach
the weight of their responsibility,
as day by day and year by year
they mould our children for their future lives.

Proverbs 2.3–8

Yes, beg for knowledge; plead for insight. Look for it as hard as you would for silver or some hidden treasure. If you do, you will know what it means to fear the Lord and you will succeed in learning about God. It is the Lord who gives wisdom; from him come knowledge and understanding. He provides help and protection for righteous, honest men. He protects those who treat others fairly, and guards those who are devoted to him. *(GNB)*

The hesitation

Jesus, I saw you in the street today,
and felt ashamed.
It was when the old woman fell,
ragged and dirty, unsteady on her feet,
lay in a heap.
And while I paused, the boy ran forward,
black jacket, crash helmet, jeans,
and picked her up,
put her worn slippers
back on her bare feet, and wiped the dirt
from her bewildered face,
led her away.

I was too late because I paused, Lord Jesus,
and you were on your feet
already.
Give me a ready heart like yours, my Jesus,
ready to pity, to comfort and to love.
Give me another chance
to prove I love you, and to run and do
what you'd have done.

Romans 7.15, 18, 24, 25

I do not understand what I do; for I don't do what I would like to do, but instead I do what I hate. I know that good does not live in me – that is, in my human nature. For even though the desire to do good is in me, I am not able to do it. Who will rescue me from this body that is taking me to death? Thanks be to God, who does this through our Lord Jesus Christ! (*GNB*)

Moving house

Lord help me to look forward,
not grievingly back.
The rooms that have been my skin, my outer self,
that I have cleaned and decorated, loved and hated,
where I have felt most truly just myself,
stand empty, hurt, betrayed.
Everything packed, dark marks where pictures hung,
heating switched off.
Even the garden looks forlorn,
waiting for other hands to care for it.

And at our journey's end there stands a shell,
empty and bleak until we bring it life.
Tomorrow our new home
will have begun to be a part of us. Not only furniture we're taking there, but all ourselves,
the bits and pieces of our lives, hobbies and toys,
tools and work-basket, dog and cat.
And more than that,

we're taking love and laughter,
the sound of voices, welcome of a home.
Lord, will the neighbours like us?
Will the schools
be able to supply our children's needs? The
    doctor, Father,
will he be kind and good at listening?
So much unknown, such loss of all
security. And yet we know
that at all journey's ends you will be there
waiting with outstretched hands to welcome us.
And by your wisdom will our house be built,
full of all precious things.

Proverbs 24.3–4

By wisdom a house is built, and by understanding it is established; by knowledge the rooms are filled with all precious and pleasant riches.

(RSV)

INDEX OF BIBLE REFERENCES

Genesis I.25 *page 29*
     21.14–17 *p. 99*

Numbers 6.24–26 *p. 51*

1 Samuel 3.26–28 *p. 85*

2 Kings 7.9 *p. 107*

1 Chronicles 4.23 *p. 21*

Job 38.22–30 *p. 101*

Psalm 4.8 *p. 69*
    12.7–8 *p. 95*
    16.5–6 *p. 109*
    23.1–3 *p. 97*
    27.4–5 *p. 9*
    31.9–10 *p. 109*
    34.1–3 *p. 11*
    34.18 *p. 53*
    46.10 *p. 13*
    65.10–11 *p. 77*
    90.1–4 *p. 37*
    92.12–15 *p. 57*
    103.15–17 *p. 87*
    118.24 *p. 29*
    121 *p. 105*
    127.3–4 *p. 41*
    145.13–14 *p. 31*

Proverbs 2.3–8 *p. 113*
    17.22 *p. 65*
    22.29 *p. 47*
    24.3–4 *p. 117*
    27. 10 *p. 93*

Song of Solomon 2.10–12 *p. 63*

Isaiah 26.3   p. 91
      40.29–31   p. 19
      46.4   p. 27
      50.4   p. 23

Jeremiah 1.6–7   p. 59

Matthew 6.20–21   p. 111
      10.29   p. 83
      11.19   p. 93
      22.2   p. 75

Mark 4.39   p. 43
      6.31–34   p. 73
      9.22–24   p. 35

Luke 5.12–13   p. 67
      10.40–42   p. 17
      15.8–9   p. 79

John 2.1–2   p. 75
      12.26   p. 21
      13.3–5   p. 71
      14.18, 23   p. 81
      14.27   p. 33
      17.3, 15   p. 45

Romans 7.15, 18, 24, 25   p. 115
      12.8   p.103

2 Corinthians 12.9   pp. 15, 21

Galatians 6.2   p. 103

1 Timothy 6.17   p. 25

Hebrews 2.18   p. 49

James 1.5–6   p. 55

Other Winston Books on the Bible, Spirituality, and Prayer

Experiencing God All Ways and Every Day
J. Norman King
#8213 $7.95

Five Gospels
An Account of How the Good News Came to Be
John C. Meagher
#8376 (cloth) $17.50
#8167 (paper) $9.95

Gospel Journey
Forty Meditations Drawn from the Life of Christ
Ernest Ferlita
#8256 $5.95

Our Story According to St. Mark
William H. Barnwell
#8215 $9.95

Out of Easter, the Gospels
Jean Hall
#8374 $3.95

The Personal Faith of Jesus
As Revealed in the Lord's Prayer
J. Neville Ward
#8258 $6.95

A Place to Start
The Bible As a Guide for Today
R.T. "Peter" Brooks
#8305 $4.95

Prayer
A Discovery of Life
Alexandra Kovats
#8361 $3.95

Prayer Making
Richard W. Chilson
#8202 $5.95

The Role of Faith in the Process of Healing
Edgar N. Jackson
#8262 $9.95

Sharing Our Biblical Story
Joseph P. Russell
#8936 $9.95

Thoughts on the Run
Glimpses of Wholistic Spirituality
Thomas E. Legere
#8277 $7.95

The Winston Commentary on the Gospels
Michael Fallon
#8257 $12.95

Available at your bookstore or from
Winston Press
430 Oak Grove
Minneapolis, Minnesota 55403